ENDANGERED MOUNTAIN ANIMALS

Dave Taylor

Toronto · Oxford · New York
Crabtree Publishing Company

ENDANGERED ANIMALS SERIES

Text and photographs by Dave Taylor

For Susan

Editor-in-chief
Bobbie Kalman

Editors
Janine Schaub
Shelagh Wallace

Photo page 26
Loretta Penny

Cover mechanicals
Diane Coderre

Design and computer layout
Antoinette "Cookie" DeBiasi

Type output
Lincoln Graphics

Color separations
ISCOA

Printer
Worzalla Publishing

Published by
Crabtree Publishing Company

350 Fifth Avenue
Suite 3308
New York
N.Y. 10118

6900 Kinsmen Court
P.O. Box 1000
Niagara Falls, ON
Canada L2E 7E7

73 Lime Walk
Headington
Oxford OX3 7AD
United Kingdom

Cataloguing in Publication Data
Taylor, Dave, 1948-
Endangered mountain animals

(The Endangered animals series)
Includes index.
ISBN 0-86505-531-9 (library bound) ISBN 0-86505-541-6 (pbk.)

1. Alpine fauna - Juvenile literature.
2. Endangered species - Juvenile literature.
3. Wildlife conservation - Juvenile literature.
I. Title. II. Series: Taylor, Dave, 1948-
The endangered animals series.

QL113.T38 1992 j591.52'909143

Contents

The world's mountains

Mountains are found on every continent. The highest are in Asia and South America, but Europe and North America have some very tall ones, too!

Mountains are created in two ways. When there is a crack in the earth's crust and lava pours out, a cone-shaped mountain, called a **volcano**, builds up. This can happen on land or under the ocean.

The other way in which mountains are formed is by the folding and cracking of the earth's crust. Large pieces of the earth's crust, called **plates**, move slowly around the earth's surface. Sometimes the plates collide. Great pressure from inside the earth causes the rocks at the edges of the plates to bend upwards. Sometimes the layers of rock crack, leaving one section jutting upwards and the other section sinking downwards. Mountain ranges that stretch for thousands of kilometers have been formed this way. They are called **fold mountains**.

Safe in high places

Mountains are rugged, difficult places for people to explore. This means that they are often the last places where farms or towns are built. For this reason, mountains offer natural protection for wildlife. Animals are safer in the mountains than they are in the grasslands or forests.

Life on the way up

The landscape and wildlife on a mountain is very different at the bottom than on the peaks. Each level of a mountain supports unique plants and wildlife. On one particular mountain, the grassy foothills may be home to grazing elk and deer. Further up, wolves and grizzly bears may stalk the pine forests, and a little higher still, small plants and dwarf trees supply food for bighorns and goats. Very few creatures live at the top's icy cliffs.

Animals in distress

In recent years, people have forced many kinds of animals to struggle for survival. Hunting, farming, and the loss of wilderness areas have made life difficult and sometimes impossible for thousands of species of animals.

Worldwide conservation groups have developed various terms to describe animals in distress. Animals that are **extinct** have not been seen in the wild for over fifty years. Animals referred to as **endangered** are likely to die out if their situation is not improved. **Threatened** animals are endangered in some areas where they live. **Rare** animals are species with small populations that may be at risk.

A concern for all animals

There is a concern for all animals living in the wild. Even if some species are not yet threatened or endangered, they may lose their lives because of pollution or loss of their homes. There is hope, however. Due to the efforts of conservation groups, many animals that once faced extinction are now surviving in healthy numbers again.

(top) The plants and animals that live on mountains must survive in a harsh environment of extreme temperatures, less oxygen, and a lot more sunshine.

(bottom) The endangered wild yak can be found in the mountains of northern Tibet, where it grazes on grass and drinks a lot of water.

(top) For many years, the red panda was the only panda known to scientists. Like its relative, the giant panda, the red panda lives high in the mountains of China, where there is a plentiful supply of bamboo—its favorite food.

(right) Golden eagles are now found only in northern mountainous regions where they are safe from human interference. They were once common throughout Europe, Asia, and North America.

The giant panda

The giant panda is well known and much loved. It is one of the rarest animals in the world! There are fewer than 1,000 pandas left in the mountains of China. Their endangered status and the affection people feel for them have made conservationists choose the panda as the international symbol of wildlife conservation.

Choosy eaters

The panda spends most of its day searching for and eating bamboo. It even has a special thumblike bone on each front paw to help it grab bamboo shoots! The panda relies almost entirely on approximately twenty types of bamboo for its food. Bamboo is a grass that lives about one hundred years and then dies. If the pandas do not move on, they will starve before the new thickets form.

Panda corridors

In the past, when one variety of bamboo died off, pandas moved to another area. Today, however, farms and towns often stand between pandas and their food. Pandas are reluctant to cross populated areas because they do not like people.

When the bamboo in an isolated region dies, all the pandas die, too. The Chinese government is setting up "panda corridors," which are protected paths that connect stranded pandas with live thickets of bamboo to ensure them of food.

Panda parks and zoos

For centuries, pandas have been hunted for their beautiful black-and-white fur. Although there are twelve parks set aside for pandas in China, **poaching** is still a problem. Poaching is the illegal killing of pandas. There are fewer than 100 pandas in captivity. These animals do not breed well in zoos.

Mothers and cubs

Mother pandas give birth to one kitten-sized cub. Panda babies are totally dependent on their mothers. It takes them three months before they can crawl and four months before they are weaned. Baby pandas stay with their mothers for at least a year and a half.

Silent and solitary

Pandas are usually quiet and like to live alone. The exceptions to this rule are mating pairs and females with young. Pandas must seek out one another in order to breed and have been heard making growls, honks, and chirps to attract possible mates. Their cry is similar to the cry of a human baby.

Length: 5-6 feet (1.5-1.8 meters)
Weight: 165-353 pounds (75-160 kilograms)
Where it lives: Central China

Some people think that the panda belongs to the raccoon family, but many scientists today feel that the panda is more bearlike. People must do everything possible to save this unique animal.

Bighorn sheep

A century ago, bighorn sheep could be found in most of the river valleys of the American plains. As these areas were settled, the sheep were forced to move to the high mountain regions. There was a time when it seemed that all the bighorn sheep would be doomed, but the creation of national parks in the United States and Canada have saved them.

The threat of disease

Today, bighorns are a common sight in national parks, but their survival is still uncertain. Recently, many have become sick and died. Scientists are hopeful that the sheep are once again gaining in number. They do worry, however, that another disease could spread and kill whole flocks in certain ranges.

Time to move!

To help prevent the death of an entire flock, herds are being captured and moved to new locations. Should a disease hit one herd, it would then not affect other herds that are farther away.

Rams that roam high

Male bighorn sheep are called **rams**. Females are called **ewes**, and youngsters are called **lambs**. Rams spend most of their year away from the ewes. They move to the highest valleys in the spring and summer, whereas the ewes and lambs stay in lower, more sheltered ones. Winter snows force the rams down to look for the females. This is their breeding season, called the **rut**.

The clash of the rut

During the rut, males fight each other to determine which are stronger. The stronger males have the choice of breeding with the best ewes. They rear up on their back legs and then charge headlong into each other as fast as they can. When their horns meet, there is a loud crash! For a second or two, both rams are knocked silly. Soon, however, the two rams charge and butt again until one of the sheep is frightened away. These encounters look like they could kill but, fortunately, rams have thick horns and tough skulls that protect them.

Mountain babies

In January, the rut is over, and the rams and ewes leave one another. In May and June, the ewes give birth to one or two lambs on narrow ledges where wolves, cougars, and bears are unlikely to hunt them. Within a few days, the lambs can run and climb almost as well as their mothers. Lambs often play with other lambs, chasing, butting heads, and leaping from rock to rock. On the dangerous cliff faces, where there is loose rock, bighorn lambs cannot afford to be unsure about their footing!

Height: 36-40 inches (91-102 centimeters)
Length: 66-73 inches (168-185 centimeters)
Weight: Female: 123-175 pounds (56-79 kilograms) Male: 125-310 pounds (57-141 kilograms)
Where they live: Rocky Mountains of North America

Bighorn sheep feed mainly on grasses but, in the southwestern part of their range, they have been known to eat shrubs and even cacti.

The split hoofs of bighorn sheep allow them to climb sheer cliffs. The hoofs are flexible, concave, and sharp-edged.

The sun bear

The sun bear is the smallest type of bear alive today. It is found in both the mountains and lowlands of Southeast Asia. The sun bear has the shortest and sleekest coat of any type of bear. Its fur ranges in color from deep brown to black, with a whitish or yellow patch on the chest area.

Claws for climbing

The sun bear's natural habitat is high in the trees of Asian forests. This small bear uses its long, thick claws for climbing and holding onto smooth bark. Sun bears are active at night, eating tree fruits, termites, small animals, birds, coconuts, and plants. During the day, they sleep in the trees in beds of branches and leaves.

Plentiful food

Sun bears do not hibernate for the winter. Bears that live in parts of the world that have winter hibernate to save their energy when food is scarce. Sun bears always have food to eat and do not have to hibernate. The climate is warm all year, and plants are constantly growing.

Bears as pets

For generations, the sun bear has been captured as a pet because it is such a gentle creature. Unfortunately, mother bears are often killed so that the cubs can be taken away. Cubs frequently die once they are no longer in their mother's care.

Killing for medicine

The greatest danger faced by the sun bear and several other varieties of bears is that they are hunted for their internal organs. The bear's **gallbladder** is used in far-eastern medicines and is worth more than its weight in gold! As a result, bears are hunted illegally and face shaky futures.

Height: 27 inches (69 centimeters)
Length: 36-54 inches (91-137 centimeters)
Weight: 50-80 pounds (23-36 kilograms)
Where it lives: Southeast Asia

The sun bear is also known by the names "honey bear," "Malay bear," and "bruang."

The bongo

The bongo is found only in the thickest parts of the African mountain rainforests. This antelope is a secretive animal that does its best to avoid people. The color of its fur resembles the pattern sunlight makes as it shines through leaves and onto the ground. This pattern **camouflages** the bongo in the forest. Older males are often black, which helps hide them in the dark jungle.

Hide and seek

Bamboo shoots grow very closely together and can make travel through a thicket next to impossible. In some spots, you cannot see more than a few steps ahead! Although the bongo does not eat bamboo, this type of forest provides the animal with excellent hiding places.

The bongo is so rarely seen that even its predator, the leopard, has difficulty hunting it. If the bongo does detect a noise with its sensitive ears, it simply moves deeper into the thicket.

Scarce food

Bongos are rare in parts of their range because food is scarce. The patches of plants upon which these antelopes feed are often small and far apart. One feeding area can only support a few bongos. For this reason, bongos live in pairs or in small groups of up to thirty members.

A dangerous diet

Scientists noted that in one part of their range in Kenya the number of bongos changed quite dramatically from year to year. One year there would be many, the next, only a few. Scientists believe that the drop in the number of this antelope may be related to its diet. There is a vine that bongos love to eat. It is a safe food most of the time, but when it is two years old, it turns poisonous! When the bongos eat the plant, they die.

The bongo is well adapted to its mountain rainforest home. It has a higher back than front, which allows it to run quickly through the trees and thickets. Its coloring camouflages it well among the dark trees.

Studied in zoos

Most of the information that scientists have learned about bongos comes from studies that were conducted in zoos. Males have been observed using their heavy horns to battle with one another. Zoo officials also know that bongos move quickly and can leap effortlessly over fences.

Height: 24-51 inches (61-130 centimeters)
Length: 100 inches (254 centimeters)
Weight: Female: 460-560 pounds (209-254 kilograms) Male: 530-890 pounds (240-404 kilograms)
Where it lives: Africa

The Andean flamingo

Flamingos used to be hunted for their beautiful feathers. Today, the major threat to these birds is the destruction of their habitats. More and more of the lakes in which the flamingos nest and catch their food are becoming polluted. Many lakes are being drained and used for farmland. Flamingos have fewer places to live.

Mountain living

There are four types of flamingos in the world. All of these birds live near lakes in huge flocks. In Africa, some flocks number over one million birds! The Andean flamingo flocks are not as large because their food is not as plentiful. Andean flamingos depend on the lakes in

the Andes Mountains in South America. They spend their whole lives at very high altitudes.

Shrimpy food

The Andean flamingo, like other flamingos, feeds on water plants and small water animals called **crustaceans**. Crustaceans are so tiny that it is hard to see them without a magnifying glass! These small shrimplike creatures can only live in lakes that have the right amount of salt. These lakes are few and far between.

Combing the water

Flamingos have tiny hairlike combs in their beaks. As the birds sweep their beaks back and forth through the water, they catch crustaceans in their combs. They suck the food off their combs and let the water drain away.

An only child

Flamingos make cuplike nests out of lake mud. Mother flamingos lay only one egg, and both parents care for the single chick. They carefully feed it until it is ready to be on its own. Flamingos take four years to become fully grown.

Height: 47 inches (120 centimeters)
Where it lives: Central Andes Mountains of South America

Flamingos eat huge amounts of red algae, which gives them their bright-pink color. They have long legs for wading in the water and combs in their beaks to help them net their dinners.

The snow leopard is also known as an **ounce.** *In summer, female ounces have from one to four cubs. Baby leopards stay with their mothers for two years before they are ready to hunt on their own. Snow leopards shed a great amount of fur in the summer in order to stay cool.*

The snow leopard

Snow leopards have beautiful smoky-gray coats with black spots. These markings allow the leopards to blend in with the rock and snow of their mountain homes. For centuries, hunters have killed snow leopards for their thick, warm winter coats. Four skins are needed to make one fur coat! Killing so many of these rare leopards has left fewer than 400 cats in the wild. Sadly, it is now their rarity that makes snow leopards the targets of hunters. Although it is illegal to sell snow-leopard skins, these hides are so valuable that many hunters are willing to risk going to jail to get one!

Clash with farmers

Like other large cats, snow leopards need large hunting ranges. They hunt alone, and many have territories that stretch up to 40 miles (64 kilometers). As more farmers move farther into remote mountain areas to graze their sheep and goats, their needs clash with those of snow leopards. Snow leopards often end up killing farm animals in order to survive because their territories are shrinking and there are fewer wild animals for prey.

Cats that purr

Snow leopards make noises similar to house cats! They cannot roar like lions or tigers—they purr instead. Their voice boxes resemble those of domestic house cats. Their lifespans are also similar. Snow leopards in captivity live approximately fifteen years, the same as house cats do. In the wild, however, their lives are much shorter because of the many dangers these wild cats face.

Expert mountain climbers

Endangered snow leopards have managed to survive by moving into some of the most remote mountain areas in the world. They have huge lungs and strong chests that enable them to breathe easily at high altitudes. They have long tails and muscular bodies that allow them to move and jump along cliffs without losing their balance. Their two front paws are heavily padded, which makes it possible for them to grip rocks firmly.

Cooperation needed

Some countries, such as Nepal, have established national parks to protect the snow leopard. The money that is earned from park tourism is given to farmers. When the snow leopard is in a protected habitat, it is less likely to hunt where cattle are grazing. Conservationists believe that other countries in the snow leopard's range should also create such areas. Without cooperation, snow leopards may not survive past the turn of the century.

Height: 24 inches (61 centimeters)
Length: (with tail) 85-95 inches (216-241 centimeters)
Weight: 50-90 pounds (23-41 kilograms)
Where it lives: Himalayan Mountains of Asia

The sacred baboon

Sacred baboons are also known as **hamadryas baboons**. Hamadryas means "living together in trees" in Greek. This is a rather misleading name because sacred baboons live on the ground in the dry, rocky mountains of the southern Sahara Desert. They used to live as far north as Egypt but are now extinct in those areas. To survive, sacred baboons have tried to live as far away as possible from people.

Ancient servants

Sacred baboons get their name from their many roles in Egyptian times. They are pictured on ancient tomb and temple walls carrying out a variety of tasks. Ancient Egyptians used these baboons as helpers and entertainers. Sometimes the baboons helped them fish, stack wood, do field work, and even serve wine at coronations!

Social monkeys

Sacred baboons are members of the monkey family. Like many monkeys, they are social animals that do not like to be alone. They live in groups, whose members care for and protect one another. Sacred-baboon groups number approximately fifteen females and youngsters and are each headed by a single male. The leader mates with the females in his group.

Family networks

Sometimes a small group of sacred baboons meets up with another group. Together, thirty or forty baboons form a **clan**. A meeting of more than two clans is called a **band**. When several bands join, the large assembly is called a **troop**. Some sacred-baboon troops may have over two hundred members!

Varied diets

Sacred baboons have extremely varied diets. In the wild, they eat all sorts of fruit, vegetables, small animals, and insects. In captivity, some sacred baboons have shown food preferences for spaghetti and even caesar salad!

Length: 35-61 inches (90-155 centimeters)
Weight: Female: 22 pounds (10 kilograms)
Male: 37 pounds (17 kilograms)
Where it lives: Ethiopia, Somalia, Saudi Arabia, and South Yemen

The sacred baboon was sacred to Toth, the ancient Egyptian god of learning.

The brown bear

Once brown bears roamed the world's prairies and plains. Today, with more and more human beings living on our planet, brown bears have been forced to live in mountain habitats to escape people. British Columbia and Alaska still have large numbers of these bears. In Europe, however, the brown bear is in danger.

The prize of hunters

Brown bears have been hunted for centuries. Several hundred years ago, Switzerland's ruler shot a bear on a hunting trip and decided to name the capital after it. Although "Berne" means bear, there is not a single bear left in all of Switzerland. In fact, there are fewer than 30 wild bears living in all of Europe! The ones that have managed to hide from people live in the mountains of Italy.

The awesome grizzly

The grizzly bear is perhaps the most famous of all brown bears. A male grizzly can weigh 900 pounds (408 kilograms) and stand 9 feet (almost 3 meters) tall! Like all brown bears, grizzlies are **omnivores**; they eat any food available. If they catch a fish, they eat it. If it is berry season, they might pick clean a whole patch! At one time, there were as many as 100,000 grizzlies in the United States.

Today, only a few hundred of these threatened bears remain south of the Canadian border. They are protected in national parks.

The big sleep

When the cold weather comes, brown bears become sluggish. They **hibernate** in dens during the winter and live off their own stores of body fat until spring arrives. During hibernation, female bears give birth to two or three cubs. At birth, cubs weigh about as much as a kitten but, by spring, they are the size of small dogs.

Yellowstone National Park officials have shot so many garbage-eating bears that people fear that the entire species may soon be gone.

Learning lessons

Cubs sometimes remain with their mothers for up to one year. During this time, mother bears teach their babies how to hunt and find the right kinds of plants to eat. Once mother bears are satisfied that the babies know their lessons, they chase their youngsters away to find their own territories. Female bears are then free to have another set of cubs.

Height: 4-5 feet (1.2-1.5 meters)
Length: 6-9 feet (1.8-2.8 meters)
Weight: Female: 265-450 pounds (120-204 kilograms) Male: 450-975 pounds (204-442 kilograms)
Where it lives: Northwest North America, the mountains of Europe, Scandinavia, and Russia

Barbary sheep

The native home of Barbary sheep extends from the highest peaks of Africa's Atlas Mountains to the Red Sea. Today, however, their range is much more limited due to overhunting for their hides and meat. In some areas, these sheep live in such isolated spots that when disease strikes, all the sheep die.

Another name for Barbary sheep is **aoudad**. *An aoudad can survive five days without water.*

Goats or sheep?

Some scientists believe that, in appearance and habit, Barbary sheep closely resemble goats. They have similar coloring, a similar tail, and a goatlike coat of long hair around their front legs. In other ways, they are like bighorn sheep. They bleat like sheep, and the males clash their horns together during the rut, just as bighorns do.

Dealing with dryness

In the mountains of North Africa, there is almost no rain. Barbary sheep are famous for their ability to survive in this arid region that has very little water. When there are no puddles or streams, these sheep get the water they need from the plants they eat and by licking morning dew off plants and rocks. When there is not enough water around for a proper bath, Barbary sheep have another way of cleaning themselves. They take mud baths to reduce the number of insects that live in their fur.

Hop across the ocean

Barbary sheep are endangered in parts of their African range. It is unlikely, however, that they will become extinct because several herds were introduced in North America. They were imported to be hunted, but they have done so well that in some places their population is greater than that of their African relatives.

Height: 35-40 inches (89-102 centimeters)
Length: 61-75 inches (155-190 centimeters)
Weight: 150-300 pounds (68-136 kilograms)
Where they live: North Africa

Barbary sheep are very agile, easily jumping from rock to rock in their mountain homes. Even baby sheep are able to run, jump, and climb within a few hours of birth.

The mountain gorilla

At the turn of the last century, scientists discovered a variety of gorilla that they had never seen before—the mountain gorilla. Until then, scientists knew of only two types of lowland gorillas. Since that time, it has taken people less than ninety years to push the mountain gorilla to the edge of extinction. There are fewer than 400 mountain gorillas left in the wild today! Although these animals are now protected, poachers still kill them for their skins and hands, which are sold as souvenirs.

A silverback's family

Mountain gorillas live in small groups of up to twenty animals. Each group is led by a male called a **silverback**. His name comes from the grayish area of fur that spreads across his otherwise jet-black coat. The silverback protects the females and youngsters in his group. Sometimes another related male helps him with his job. When the youngsters reach adulthood at about fifteen years of age, they move on to form their own groups.

Eating and nesting

Mountain gorillas spend most of their time eating fruits and plants. They move slowly through the mountain forests, nibbling on leaves, branches, and bark. Adults rest in the afternoons, while the young wrestle, swing, and play. In the evening, all the gorillas make nests on the ground out of branches and leaves. Their long hair keeps them warm during the cold mountain nights.

Wildlife research

A great deal is known about the mountain gorilla due to the efforts of a wildlife researcher named Dian Fossey. Fossey spent thirteen years living side by side with gorillas in the wild. She felt they needed protection from the poachers who hunted them. It is believed that Fossey was murdered by an angry gorilla poacher.

Money for survival

Today, Fossey's work is carried on by the "Mountain Gorilla Project." The project offers tours to small groups of people who want to observe wild gorillas. Tourist dollars are used to support gorilla research. Some of the money is given to local farmers. Conservationists hope that farmers who receive an income from the money earned from gorillas will be more likely to protect these animals. No one is certain of the effect that tourists will have on the mountain gorillas but, so far, the "Mountain Gorilla Project" has succeeded in increasing the number of gorillas by 100!

Height: Female: 54-60 inches (137-152 centimeters) Male: 66-72 inches (168-183 centimeters)
Weight: Female: 200 pounds (91 kilograms) Male: 310-400 pounds (141-181 kilograms)
Where it lives: Mountains of Zaire, Rwanda, and Uganda

In captivity, gorillas can live to be fifty years old. In the wild, they seldom survive past thirty-five.

Dangers to mountain habitats

Many people think of mountains as isolated places that will last forever. This is far from true. Mountains are constantly being worn away or **eroded** by water, wind, and extreme changes in temperature. Over millions of years, tall mountains can be reduced to rolling hills! It is people, however, that cause the quickest and most drastic changes to mountain habitats.

Changing the face of a mountain

Logging companies that remove all the trees from a mountain without replanting any can destroy that mountain. The thin layer of soil that used to be held in place by trees is quickly washed away by rain. A forested slope can turn into a barren cliff face in less than a year. Other human activities also destroy mountain habitats. Mining, farming, hydro-electric projects,

ranching, road-building, hunting, and even mountain-climbing can threaten the plants and animals that live in mountains. around them are destroyed or changed. Some animals are being pushed farther and farther up a mountain to survive.

A last refuge

Mountains are among the last refuges for endangered animals. Many kinds of creatures have learned to live in mountain areas to escape people. Some have had their natural habitats taken from them. Others are left stranded in mountainous areas when the regions

Mountain animals depend on scarce food supplies and must live in harsh climates. When their fragile world is upset by people, their existence is threatened.

Also known as the Andean bear, the spectacled bear is the only species of the bear family found in South America. It lives mainly in the forests of the Andes Mountains. Its name comes from the whitish "spectacles" that encircle its eyes.

Taking a stand

Everyone can help in the preservation of mountain habitats by being respectful of nature and by refusing to participate in any activities that will endanger these areas. If you know of a mountain habitat that needs protection, perhaps you and your classmates can find out what can be done and inform others. You could campaign to have more land set aside for mountain parks and wildlife reserves.

Glossary

altitude The elevation above sea level
Andes Mountains A mountain range in western South America
antelope An animal that chews cud and has unbranched horns and split hoofs
arid Dry; having little rainfall
Atlas Mountains A mountain range in northwestern Africa
barren Having little or no plant life
camouflage An animal's behavior or appearance that hides it by making it blend into its surroundings
conservation Protection from loss, harm, or waste, especially of natural resources, such as wildlife
crustacean A group of animals that have hard shells and jointed bodies and that live in water and breathe through gills
cud The barely chewed food that some animals bring up from their first stomach back into their mouth for a thorough second chewing
distress A condition of danger or need
earth's crust The hard outer layer of the earth
endanger To threaten with extinction
erosion The gradual wearing away of the earth's surface by water, wind, and glaciers
foothill A low hill at the bottom of a mountain or mountain range
gallbladder A small sac attached to the liver in which bile, a liquid that helps digestion, is stored
habitat The natural environment of a plant or animal
hibernate To be in an inactive state
international Between or among countries
lava Hot liquid rock ejected from a volcano
national park An area of land maintained for public use by the government
omnivore An animal that eats all kinds of food
ounce Another name for the snow leopard
plates Large pieces of the earth's crust that move slowly on the earth's surface. Colliding plates cause earthquakes.
poacher A person who hunts illegally
predator An animal that captures and eats other animals
prey An animal that is hunted by another animal for food
range An area over which animals roam and find food
Red Sea The sea between Saudi Arabia and northeastern Africa
remote Secluded or out of the way
rut The season in which animals court and breed
species A group of related plants or animals that can produce young together
status Position or rank
thicket A dense growth of shrubs or bushes
unique Unusual, rare, or noteworthy
volcano A cone-shaped mountain built up out of the lava that is ejected from its center

Index

3 4 5 6 7 8 9 0 Printed in USA 1 0 9 8 7 6 5 4 3